Classroom Plays for Social Studies
Early America

Author .................L.E. McCullough
Illustrator ....Mark Mason
Editor ....Kathy Rogers
Cover Design ....Leanne Milliken

EP241 • ©2003 Edupress, Inc.™ • P.O. Box 883 • Dana Point, CA 92629
www.edupressinc.com
ISBN 1-56472-241-4
Printed in USA

Introduction

The plays included in this book are interactive learning aids designed to make history and cultural study come alive for your students. You'll quickly find that dramatizing a lesson stimulates your students to do more research and get more mentally involved with the subject, enhancing your efforts to impart basic knowledge to students, and inspiring them to discover more about the subject on their own.

It is a teacher's challenge to create a collaborative, personalized learning environment to address students' varying "learning intelligences." Drama, with its inherent capacity to tap into and synthesize a wide range of skills and expressive modes, is a highly effective way of achieving this goal. You don't need to be a trained theatre specialist to make use of these plays. You only have to know how to read! And, of course, you'll find the ability to channel your students' exuberance and enthusiasm into orderly collaborative expression very handy—but you have that skill as a teacher, anyway.

Consider these plays as foundations and stepping-off points for further research and learning by your students. Although each play script is self-contained and based on actual curriculum material, the format allows for additional information you might want to insert. Additionally, the activities of making sets and costumes allows you to combine with studies in other disciplines: science, language, dance, music, geography, and social studies.

Decorate the set with architecture, plants, and art objects specific to that region. If you are a music teacher and want to add songs and music to any of the plays, go ahead and make it a class project by organizing a chorus or having students select appropriate recordings from the host culture to play before and after the performance. These plays are an excellent vehicle for getting other members of the school and community involved in your project. Maybe there are ethnic dance troupes or performers of ethnic music in your area; ask them to give a special concert or lecture when you present the play. Utilize the talents of local school or youth orchestra members to play incidental music. Get the school art club to paint scrims and backdrops. See if a senior citizens' group might volunteer time to sew costumes.

Realizing that many performing groups may have limited technical and space resources, the sets, costumes, and props listed here are minimal. However, if you do have the ability to build a Powhatan hunting lodge or a scale model Independence Hall—go for it! Adding more music and dance and visual arts and crafts into the production involves more students and makes your play a genuinely multi-media event. Similarly, only basic stage directions have been supplied. Blocking is really the province of the director; once you get the play up and moving, feel free to suit cast and action to the experience level of actors. When figuring out how to stage these plays, follow the venerable UYI Method—Use Your Imagination.

Visual art sources for adding authenticity to your costumes and props abound in books, filmstrips, and on the Internet. For example, there are numerous reconstructions of the Jamestown Colony's buildings and of the Valley Forge camp site. Dozens of books with examples of colonial and Native American architecture and clothing are available in local libraries. Having students explore this dimension of material helps deepen their understanding of what it was like to live in that period. The use of the plays in this book is a great way for students to explore ancient history and see the world through the eyes of the people who lived at the dawn of American history. And you, the teacher, can proudly add "Director/Producer" to your long list of ad hoc/pro bono classroom job titles!

Break a leg!

Getting Ready

What kind of production shall we do?

The plays in this book can be presented in a number of different ways, depending on the interests and skill level of your class.

• **Classroom Theater**—Some students are more comfortable appearing in classroom performances before a small group of their classmates or another class. This method requires minimal set decoration, although costumes do add interest and fun.

• **Dramatic Reading**—The performers give a dramatic reading of the script, complete with gestures and movement. This approach requires a minimum of rehearsal time and simplifies preparation, as there is no need for sets or costumes.

• **Puppet Theater**—The use of puppets can be entertaining and comfortable for students too shy to appear in front of a group.

• **Stage Performance**—Where a stage or auditorium is available, this type of performance can be exciting and fun for a student group to produce.

Assigning Parts

The plays have been written with large casts to get as many students involved as possible. Feel free to add or subtract "extra" characters as needed to suit your classroom population. Except for a few lead roles where a sense of audience expectation more or less demands that the gender of the actor and character match, feel free to mix boys and girls in supporting roles as your student demographic dictates.

Not all participants in a play must be actors. There are plenty of "behind-the-scenes" jobs for everyone.

Announcer—This person introduces the play and players to the audience.

Understudies—These people learn and rehearse one or more parts, being prepared to perform if another player is absent.

Stage Manager—In a larger production, this person raises the curtain and is in charge of sound effects.

Property Master—This person takes care of props and costumes.

Playbill Writer and Illustrator—This person creates a program to distribute to the audience.

Setting the Stage

Even a classic stage presentation of your play can offer several variations. You can keep it very simple by using an open corner of the classroom as a stage, or having the students perform in the center of the classroom with the audience seated around them. If you want to give the impression of a true stage, you can hang up a sheet to act as a curtain. It might be fun for the class to paint a background scene, or "scrim," on a sheet or large pieces of cardboard. Consider using a sheltered outdoor area for your performance.

The First Read-Through

Pass out copies of the script you have chosen, and read aloud as the students read along silently. Explain how tone can change the meaning of the lines they are reading, and follow with an example. Have students practice reading lines with emphasis or meaning.

Rehearsals

Keep rehearsals relatively short, and keep the mood relaxed. For the first rehearsal, do a dramatic reading of the script, having each actor highlight his or her individual lines. Once the actors are comfortable with their parts, do a walk-through. Use the scripts, but block out some movements for the scene. Introduce the concept of stage position, explaining that these positions are from the point of view of the actor facing the audience.

As rehearsals continue, try a rehearsal without scripts, adding gestures. Your final rehearsal will be a dress rehearsal, with props. Try to let the actors get through the entire dress rehearsal without interruption, as if they were performing before an audience. Reassure your players that the purpose of the play is to have fun.

Costumes

Visual art sources for adding authenticity to your costumes and props abound in books, filmstrips, and on the Internet. Dozens of books with examples of early American architecture and clothing are available in local libraries.

Suggestions for simple costumes are included in this book. Suggestions for enhancing the basic costume are offered in the introduction of each play; it's up to you to decide how elaborate you wish to make the costumes. Suggestions for simple props are also included, as well as a few more elaborate ideas for dressing the set for a larger production.

Costume Basics

Suggestions for authentic-looking costumes can be found in the **Costumes** section of the introduction to each play. However, if you have the time and resources for only very basic costumes, the suggestions below will be helpful in creating easy costumes that can be embellished or changed to suit your needs.

Girls

1. Borrow long, full skirts and aprons.
2. Fold a 36-inch (1 m) square of fabric in half diagonally. Wrap around shoulders, securing with a safety pin in front.
3. Cover two 2-inch (5 cm) squares of cardboard with aluminum foil and attach to shoes.

Boys

1. Roll long pant legs up to just below the knee and secure with a rubber band.
2. Wear long sports socks and secure under edges of pant legs.
3. Cover two 2-inch (5 cm) squares of cardboard with aluminum foil and attach to shoes.

Pocahontas and John Smith: Saving the Virginia Colony

Summary:

In 1607, the Powhatan girl Pocahontas saves the struggling Jamestown colony by convincing her father to spare the life of Captain John Smith.

Historical Background:

Jamestown, Virginia, was the first permanent English settlement in North America. It was a small colony threatened by disease, starvation, and attacks from the local Native American tribes who saw the Europeans as invaders. After the first year, only 38 of the original 105 colonists survived.

Jamestown would have vanished completely except for the aid given by Pocahontas, daughter of a powerful local chieftain. Curious and compassionate by nature, Pocahontas befriended the colonists and helped them get food from friendly tribes. She personally intervened to save the lives of Captain John Smith and several colonists. In 1614, Pocahontas married an Englishman named John Rolfe; they had a son, Thomas, who became a wealthy tobacco planter in Virginia. Descendants of Pocahontas and the Rolfes number in the hundreds of thousands and include U.S. Senator John Randolph (1773-1833), Edith Wilson (the wife of President Woodrow Wilson), Mrs. Robert E. Lee, Mayor John Lindsay of New York, and the entertainer Wayne Newton.

Pocahontas visited England in 1616 and met many of the great political and literary figures of the day. She caught pneumonia and died at age 21. She is buried in England, where she is commemorated by several monuments. John Smith lived until 1631 and wrote several books about his many adventures. He also recorded a dictionary of several hundred words in the Powhatan language, which is no longer spoken.

Pre- or Post-Play Activities:

• What Native American tribes once lived in your region? Make a timeline of the different tribes and their history in your locality; if any members of that tribe still live nearby, ask if they will send a representative to speak to your class about their culture and history.

• Suppose you were planning to start a colony on the moon. What sort of buildings would you need? What sort of supplies would you take? What sort of workers would you want? Make a drawing of the colony and its living and working structures.

• Pocahontas and John Smith were curious about each other's culture. About what culture besides your own would you like to know more? Which aspect would you choose to learn first—language, music, art, clothing, sports, etc.?

• Jamestown was named in honor of King James I of England; Virginia was named after Queen Elizabeth I of England, who was often called "the Virgin Queen." Make a list of several towns in your county and find out how they came to be named.

Cast: 21 actors, including at least 10 boys (○) and 7 girls (+)

Pocahontas (+)

Chief Powhatan (○)

Lady De La Warr (+)

John Ratcliffe (○)

John Martin (○)

George Cassen (○)

Thomas Emry (○)

3 Powhatan Women (+)

Captain John Smith of 1617 (○)

Captain John Smith of 1607 (○)

George Percy (○)

Edward Wingfield (○)

Ponnoiske, Powhatan's Wife (+)

Powhatan's Priest (+)

John Robinson (○)

4 Powhatan Warriors

Stage Set:

No set is required; however, if desired, a scrim could be mounted behind the stage or off to the side to show slides of Native Americans, colonial English settlers, the Virginia wilderness, etc.

Props:

- 4 pouches of corn and fish
- Small, hardback book such as a prayer book
- Compass
- Flintlock pistol

- 3 bowls
- Spear
- Tomahawk
- Bow

- Manacles
- Rope
- Club
- Sword

Costumes:

John Smith wears a loose white shirt, brown vest and breeches, a cape, and knee-length boots; workers like George Cassen, Thomas Emry, and John Robinson wear gray or brown shirts, vests, breeches of coarse, homespun linen and canvas, knee-length socks, boots, and small berets or cloth caps. The dress of gentlemen like George Percy, John Ratcliffe, John Martin, and Edward Wingfield is also a white shirt, jerkin, and breeches, but more colorful. They may wear plumed hats and leather shoes with silver buckles. Powhatan and Powhatan Warriors wear buckskin-style shirts and leggings with moccasins, and blue or white paint streaks on their faces. Pocahontas, Ponnoiske, Powhatan's Priest, and Powhatan Women wear apron-like dresses, fringed at the edges. Ponnoiske and Powhatan's Priest wear blue-colored mantles with feathers. Lady De La Warr dresses as an upper-class English aristocrat—long dark gown with a white lace collar and a fan.

Pronunciation Guide:

Ahone — A-**ho**-ne (God)

aspami — as-pa-**mee** (earth)

netab — **ne**-tab (friend)

Ponnoiske — Po-no-**is**-kay

tangoa — tan-go-**a** (give it to me)

Algonkian — Al-**gon**-kee-an

bocuttaw — bo-cut-**aw** (flame)

Pocahontas — Po-ca-**hon**-tas

Powhatan — Pow-**hat**-an

Staging Helps

Native American Buckskin Shirt or Dress

The basic costume for the Native American characters begins with a "buckskin" shirt or dress.

Materials

- Extra large T-shirt, beige or white
- Scissors

Directions

1. If using a white T-shirt, dye the shirt a tan color by soaking it in cold tea. Wring out the shirt and allow to dry.
2. Use scissors to cut the hem of the shirt at one-inch (2.5 cm) intervals to make fringe.
3. Complete the costume with feathered headbands and armbands, or embellishments of your choice.

Tomahawk

Native American tomahawks were not only weapons. They were used as tools and were a symbol of peace during ceremonies. Here are directions for a Club Tomahawk.

Materials

- Cardboard, cut 4x24 inches (10x61 cm)
- Tempera paint in a variety of colors
- Feathers (real or cut from construction paper)
- Paintbrush
- Scissors
- Glue

Directions

1. Cut cardboard into a shape that is slightly tapered, as shown in illustration at right.
2. Paint both sides of the cardboard with Native American designs.
3. Glue feathers to ends and sides of tomahawk.

Pocahontas and John Smith: Saving the Virginia Colony

(As the play begins, Captain John Smith stands at down left. SOUND: church bells tolling, subside.)

Captain John Smith of 1617: *(addresses audience, points behind him)* All the noise is coming from St. George's Church. Very old church, even by English standards. It has been here nearly six hundred years here at Gravesend-by-the-Sea, built when Saxon kings ruled this island. A lot of funerals have gone on inside those gray stone walls. Today, a young woman of twenty-one years is being laid to rest.

(Lady De La Warr enters from left, dabbing at her eyes with a handkerchief.)

Captain John Smith of 1617: Lady De La Warr! Greetings and salutations! *(bows deeply)*

Lady De La Warr: I am so sorry for your loss, Captain Smith. I know that Lady Rebecca was a good friend.

Captain John Smith of 1617: She was more than a friend to me. She was a friend to the people of England. Maybe the best they have ever had.

Lady De La Warr: The headstone is quite handsome. More tribute than many a poor woman receives after a life of toil.

Captain John Smith of 1617: Simple and elegant, just as she was herself.

Lady De La Warr: "Mrs. John Rolfe, Wife of John Rolfe, Merchant."

Captain John Smith of 1617: Yes. But to me, she will always be known as "Pocahontas, Princess of Virginia."

(Captain John Smith of 1607 enters from right between two English soldiers, John Ratcliffe and John Martin; his hands are bound with a manacle.)

Captain John Smith of 1617: It was the tenth of June, the year 1607, in the reign of our monarchs James and Anne. Our party of 105 men and boys had landed at Jamestown one month before. I, however, had been accused on the voyage of inciting mutiny and was only now being released from the stockade. Not exactly a grand welcome for a soldier who had fought for the glory of England in a dozen wars around the world!

(Edward Wingfield enters from right and stands before Smith of 1607.)

Edward Wingfield: Captain John Smith, you are hereby released from custody. And you are sworn to the colony council by authority of me—Edward Wingfield, council president. *(nods to John Ratcliffe and John Martin)* I do so as witnessed by council members John Ratcliffe and John Martin.

(Edward Wingfield releases the manacle from Smith.)

John Ratcliffe & John Martin: We do so witness.

Captain John Smith of 1607: I am honored—*(rubs hands)* and relieved—to finally come to enjoy the full measure of your hospitality. But from what I see of conditions here at the colony, honor and hospitality are not going to keep us from starving or from being destroyed by the natives.

Edward Wingfield: Your reputation as a soldier is well known, Captain. But you will find military bluster of little use here in Virginia. Political skills, such as those I possess, are more in demand.

John Ratcliffe: The lands along the Atlantic Coast from Chesapeake Bay all the way to North Carolina are ruled by Chief Powhatan, leader of the Powhatan tribe.

John Martin: We estimate that Powhatan's kingdom covers more than eighty-five hundred square miles and includes nearly thirty different tribes—more than nine thousand people altogether.

Captain John Smith of 1607: How many of those are warriors?

John Ratcliffe: Possibly three thousand.

Captain John Smith of 1607: We are outnumbered, then, by thirty-to-one? I have faced higher odds.

John Ratcliffe: Furthermore, Powhatan's kingdom is supported by taxes from his subjects. He collects a part of all the fish, crops, animal skins, copper, and pearls they collect.

John Martin: And he has installed his relatives to rule each tribe, thus ensuring their loyalty.

Captain John Smith of 1607: It sounds as if these so-called savages are as well-organized as any European kingdom! I wonder why they do not simply march in and wipe us out? No one seems to have bothered to build any sort of fortification!

Edward Wingfield: Because the Powhatan admire us. They are fascinated by our buildings, our weapons, our tools, even our clothing. Like children, they are bemused by trinkets. Why, they trade us a month's worth of corn for a handful of glass beads!

Captain John Smith of 1607: When they see they can walk in and take what they want without asking, they will no longer bother to trade.

Edward Wingfield: The Jamestown colony must succeed, Captain. We must stop the spread of French and Spanish colonies in America. We must find gold for the royal treasury. And we must convert these Indians to our Anglican faith.

(George Percy enters from right.)

Edward Wingfield: Here comes George Percy. He will acquaint you with the grounds. God save the king!

(Edward Wingfield exits right followed by John Ratcliffe and John Martin.)

Captain John Smith of 1607: What is our situation at present?

George Percy: Grim, sir. Half the colony suffer from fever. The other half are weakened by lack of food. While you were in stockade, fifteen men died, five from attacks by the natives.

Captain John Smith of 1607: We have less than a hundred able-bodied men?

George Percy: *(counts off on fingers)* We have six carpenters, a blacksmith, a barber, a chaplain, a tailor, two bricklayers, a mason, two surgeons, twelve laborers, and forty-eight gentlemen.

Captain John Smith of 1607: What sort of labor does a "gentleman" perform?

George Percy: The gentlemen, sir, are here to protect the interest of the Virginia Company. They perform no labor at all. Besides, the planting season is almost over. We have only the food the Indians give us.

Captain John Smith of 1607: This is madness. I call a meeting of the council!

(John Ratcliffe, John Martin, George Cassen, Thomas Emry, and John Robinson enter from right, gather around Smith and Percy at down center; Smith mimes a vigorous speech.)

Captain John Smith of 1617: It was discovered that our esteemed president, Edward Wingfield, had been secreting supplies of food and drink for his own use. In fact, he had attempted to take our one remaining ship, the *Discovery*, and take flight with it back to

England, abandoning the colony. A quick vote was taken, and a new president was elected.

John Ratcliffe: All hail Captain John Smith!

Martin, Cassen, Emry, Robinson & Percy: Huzzah!

Captain John Smith of 1607: Our choice is clear. We must work or we shall starve. Each colonist is required to spend four hours per day farming. When you have made provisions to eat, then you may look for gold.

John Martin: But, Captain, I am an English gentleman!

Captain John Smith of 1607: Here in Virginia, you are an English well-digger. Pick three others and dig a well deep enough to serve five times our number. George Cassen?

George Cassen: Here, sir.

Captain John Smith of 1607: Take four men and clear thirty acres of land on the high ridge for growing corn. John Robinson?

John Robinson: Here, Captain.

Captain John Smith of 1607: You and Ratcliffe and Emry organize a crew to fell trees and build a blockhouse at the colony entrance.

John Robinson: Very good, sir. But why, sir?

Captain John Smith of 1607: Why? To safeguard the few supplies Wingfield did not steal.

(Martin, Cassen, Emry, Robinson, and Ratcliffe exit right, muttering.)

Captain John Smith of 1607: Look sharp, men. If you want to live to see the first frost of winter, you'd best show some spirit. Percy?

George Percy: Yes, Captain?

Captain John Smith of 1607: How much food do we truly have left?

George Percy: Not enough to last the month, I am afraid.

(Pocahontas and 3 Powhatan Women enter from right bearing pouches of corn and fish, which they place at Smith and Percy's feet.)

Captain John Smith of 1607: Who are these young women bringing corn and fish?

George Percy: They are from Powhatan's camp. Their leader is the tall girl, Pocahontas, the chieftain's daughter. They have been bringing us fresh game and meal for several days.

(Pocahontas and 3 Powhatan Women exit right; Pocahontas turns and looks at Smith;

she places her left hand over her heart and raises her right arm; Smith awkwardly returns the gesture; Pocahontas smiles and exits.)

Captain John Smith of 1607: Remarkable. They shoot arrows at us in the morning and give us food in the afternoon. What did you say her name was?

George Percy: Pocahontas. I have no idea what it means.

Captain John Smith of 1607: Why don't you?

George Percy: Because they are savages, sir. Who cares what their names mean?

Captain John Smith of 1607: Simply good manners, Percy. As our hosts in this New World, they allow us to survive at their will. Wouldn't it be a good idea to get better acquainted?

(George Percy shrugs and exits right, taking the pouches.)

Captain John Smith of 1617: I soon learned that in the Algonkian language, Pocahontas means "Bright Stream Between Two Hills." I learned many words from the young Indian princess, including the meaning of that gesture she made upon our first meeting.

(Pocahontas stands at down right and repeats her earlier gesture of placing her left hand over her heart and raising her right arm.)

Pocahontas: "I am your friend. I will keep my promise."

(Pocahontas crosses to Smith of 1607, who shows her a book; she leafs through the pages and is absorbed and fascinated.)

Captain John Smith of 1617: Pocahontas likewise learned many English words. A young woman of around twelve years, she was curious and highly intelligent. Interested not just in taking trinkets but in learning how we made our tools, crafted our buildings, even how we worshipped our God. She came to visit the colony often, always bringing food or some aid from friendly tribes, showing us how to plant corn and yams, teaching us how to use native plants to make medicine that cured our constant fever. After many such visits, I felt toward her as if she were my own daughter.

(Pocahontas crosses to exit right with book; stops, turns, speaks to Smith of 1607.)

Pocahontas: *Netab.* Friend. *(exits)*

Captain John Smith of 1617: As winter came on, even the kindness of Pocahontas failed to ensure the survival of Jamestown. We buried fifty men that fall, and the rest of us barely made do on sturgeon and sea crabs. One cold, rainy day in mid-December, I left the colony with a small party in search of wild game.

(Smith of 1607, Cassen, Robinson, and Emry enter from right, peering about warily.)

Captain John Smith of 1617: A short way upriver, our boat became stuck fast on a sandbar. We were forced to disperse.

John Robinson: We won't get loose until daybreak, I'm afraid.

Captain John Smith of 1607: Cassen, you stay here and guard the boat. Robinson and Emry, follow me and see if we can find something to eat.

(Cassen sits on ground as Smith, Robinson, and Emry exit right; 3 Powhatan Warriors enter from up right, sneak up on Cassen, attack and kill him, drag him offstage up right; Smith, Robinson, and Emry enter from right.)

Thomas Emry: Captain, we've been marching for hours. Can we not get some sleep?

John Robinson: Please, captain. We'll make camp in that glen. *(points offstage right)*

Captain John Smith of 1607: Very well. I shall scout the perimeter.

(Emry and Robinson exit right as Smith cautiously peers around stage; SOUND: gunshots, war whoops, screams of Emry and Robinson; Smith crouches, readies his pistol and sword; 4 Powhatan Warriors enter from up right; Smith shoots Powhatan #1, tries to fight off the other two but is subdued and held at spear point by Powhatan Warriors #2 and #3.)

Captain John Smith of 1607: I am a captain. A chief. You must take me to your chief.

(3 Powhatan Warriors hesitate; Powhatan Warrior #4 raises tomahawk.)

Captain John Smith of 1607: Wait!

(Smith takes out a compass and shows it to Warriors; they are intrigued and gaze in awe.)

Captain John Smith of 1607: Compass. Com-pass. Very good for chief. Earth—*aspami* … earth and skies … sun, moon, stars … all inside compass.

Powhatan Warrior #3: *Tangoa! (points to compass)*

(Smith hesitates; Powhatan Warrior #3 seizes compass.)

Powhatan Warrior #3: *Tangoa!*

(Powhatan Warriors #2 and #4 hustle Smith offstage right, followed by Powhatan Warrior #3 playing with compass.)

Captain John Smith of 1617: I was kept prisoner in a small village, yet treated fairly well. My belief was that I was being prepared for a sacrifice.

After several days, I was taken to the camp of Chief Powhatan himself. There, I would learn my final fate.

(Chief Powhatan enters from up right followed by Ponnoiske, Powhatan's Priest, and 3 Powhatan Women, who each carry a bowl; the group gathers at down center with Ponnoiske standing to the right of Chief Powhatan, Powhatan's Priest standing to his left, 3 Powhatan Women kneel at down right, placing bowls on ground.)

Powhatan:	Bring forth the Englishman.
Powhatan's Priest:	Bring forth the Englishman!
Powhatan Women:	Hi-yeeeeee!
Powhatan:	Let the feast begin.
Powhatan's Priest:	Let the feast begin!

(Smith of 1607, hands tied with rope, is brought in from right by 4 Powhatan Warriors; he stands before Powhatan.)

Captain John Smith of 1617: I was surrounded by several hundred warriors. Powhatan's Priest was leading the ritual, and several maidens knelt with what I took to be ceremonial bowls. I was convinced this was to be a blood sacrifice.

Powhatan Women: *Ahone! Ahone!*

Captain John Smith of 1617: My conviction grew stronger as I heard the crowd chant the Powhatan words for "God" and "flame."

Powhatan Women: *Bocuttaw! Bocuttaw!*

(Powhatan raises his right hand and chanting stops; Powhatan Warriors #1 and #2 take Smith and lay him flat on his back; Powhatan's Priest takes club and stands over Smith, looking to Powhatan for a sign to attack Smith, who stares straight at Powhatan's Priest.)

Powhatan: Hyaa!

(Powhatan's Priest raises club; Pocahontas rushes in from right, throws herself over Smith and holds out her arm to stave off a blow.)

Pocahontas: No!

(Powhatan's Priest freezes, looks to Powhatan.)

Powhatan: Hyaa!

Pocahontas: Father, do not harm this man! He is my friend! A friend to our people!

(Powhatan motions with a wave of his hand for Powhatan's Priest to step back;

Pocahontas rises and helps Smith to his feet.)

Powhatan: It is my daughter's wish to spare this man's life?

Pocahontas: It is my wish.

Powhatan: Let all who hear know Powhatan is a powerful chief. He is powerful enough to hear the wishes of his daughter and grant them.

Powhatan's Priest: Powhatan is a powerful chief!

Powhatan: Englishman, we are now friends.

Captain John Smith of 1607: Am I free to go?

Pocahontas: You will become a member of our tribe. My father will adopt you as his son.

Captain John Smith of 1607: Then I suppose I shall stay for the feast after all.

(Powhatan's Priest leads the group offstage right.)

Lady De La Warr: That is a stirring tale, Captain.

Captain John Smith of 1617: Yes, my lady. And when I returned to Jamestown, a ship from England had just arrived with fresh supplies. The colony was saved.

Lady De La Warr: Thanks be to God!

Captain John Smith of 1617: And to Pocahontas. I left Jamestown the following year. Troubles with Powhatan continued, and six years later, Pocahontas stepped forth to save the colony once more— this time by marrying young John Rolfe.

Lady De La Warr: Their marriage made peace between the tribes and the colonists.

Captain John Smith of 1617: She was the instrument that preserved the colony from death, famine, and utter confusion.

Lady De La Warr: Her story must be told. You must write a book, Captain, and set down your adventures for all the world to read.

Captain John Smith of 1617: I shall do my utmost. And I swear upon this grave, as long as there is a Virginia, the deeds of Pocahontas will not be forgotten!

CURTAIN

Daily Life in Colonial America

Summary:

Explore the life of a typical New England farm family in 1704, highlighting the need for self-sufficiency and interdependence with discussion of the significant role children played in the household economy.

Historical Background:

People who lived in Colonial America brought very few objects with them from overseas. Nearly everything they owned they made or paid someone they knew to make for them; furniture, clothing, medicine, houses, schoolbooks, and cooking utensils were all made by hand from materials and ingredients that grew or were found nearby. Children were seen as an important part of the family's effort to make a successful life in the New World.

Pre- or Post-Play Activities:

• Re-create your classroom as a New England classroom in the year 1704. What would the building look like? What would be the sources of heat and light and water? Would you have a desk? What writing and reading materials would you have available? Would everyone have books of their own?

• Draw the types of houses (inside and outside) farmers lived in during the early 1700s in New England. Make a list of household objects that would have been in the kitchen, parlor, and bedroom.

• Make a chart of foods that would have been available to a New England farm family in the early 1700s. Where would they have gotten their food? How would they have prepared it?

• Think of some chores children do today that children did in 1704; would you do them the same way then as you do now? What would be different?

Cast: 8 actors, including at least 4 boys (○) and 4 girls (+)

Hannah Holcomb, Age 11 (+)
Joshua Holcomb, Jr., Age 9 (○)
Sarah Holcomb, Age 6 (+)
Mrs. Mary Holcomb, Mother (+)

Ruth Holcomb, Age 10 (+)
Timothy Holcomb, Age 8 (○)
Mr. Joshua Holcomb, Father (○)
Mr. Murray, Schoolmaster (○)

Stage Set:

At right is a straw-stuffed mattress; at center is a fireplace with a straight-backed wooden chair, a small food preparation table, a larger eating table, a smaller straight-backed wooden chair; at left is a bench and a teacher's writing desk.

Props:

- Fireplace poker
- Bread dough
- Cooking pot
- 2-3 pieces of firewood
- Sewing needle
- Ladle
- 2 aprons
- Hornbook **

- 2 trenchers *
- Pie pan
- Serving pot
- Water dipper
- Darning needle
- 7 spoons
- 7 tin cups
- Washing pan

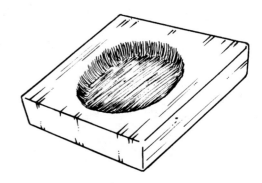

* A trencher was a square slab of wood with a hole scooped out of the middle for food; this served as a combination bowl and plate.

** A hornbook was the Colonial child's schoolbook; it was a paddle-shaped piece of wood upon which a single page of text was glued; a thin sheet of yellowish, see-through animal horn laminated the paper, protecting the page.

Costumes:

The female characters wear long woolen dresses of red, green, or blue, with white linen caps (clouts) or scarves that come over their ears. Male characters wear long-sleeved blue or green shirts, woolen or leather jackets (doublets), brown or black breeches, and knit stocking caps. All characters wear clog shoes. Females keep head coverings and scarves on at all times; male characters take off head coverings in school.

Staging Helps

It's easy to create a stage setting that looks like the interior of a colonial home!

Fireplace

Tape rectangular construction paper bricks to the back wall of the set. Leave an opening in the center. Cut a large black kettle from paper and "hang" it in the opening.

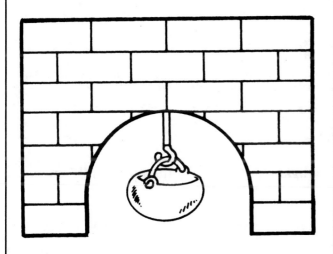

Mattresses

Stuff old pillowcases or burlap sacks with newspaper strips.

Grandfather Clock

Sketch and paint a replica of a grandfather clock on butcher paper. Cut it out and tape it on the wall of the set.

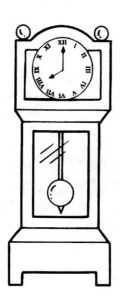

Tables & Chairs

Set plywood on two sawhorses. Use small barrels, ice cream cartons, and blocks of wood or masonry for chairs.

Daily Life in Colonial America

(As the play begins, a SOUND IS HEARD OFFSTAGE: dripping water from a leaky roof. A voice is heard offstage left.)

Ruth Holcomb (O.S.): Not again! When is this rain going to stop!

(Ruth Holcomb enters from left, sleepily rubbing her eyes; Mrs. Holcomb enters from right, holding a candle.)

Mrs. Holcomb: What is the matter, Ruth?

Ruth Holcomb: Mother, the roof is leaking again! And it woke me up from the most wonderful dream!

Mrs. Holcomb: It is almost an hour before sunrise. Time you were up to start your chores.

Ruth Holcomb: Can father fix the leak?

Mrs. Holcomb: Father is already out in the field harnessing the oxen for plowing. The roof will have to wait until tonight.

Ruth Holcomb: I can hardly wait until our new house is ready. Imagine—living in a house with three rooms!

Mrs. Holcomb: That is enough complaining, Ruth. Go get a bucket from the yard and put it under the leak. Joshua can stuff some straw in the ceiling. Now let us clear this keeping room so I can get breakfast ready.

(Ruth and Mrs. Holcomb move the bed upstage; Hannah Holcomb enters from right, tying an apron, and addresses audience.)

Hannah Holcomb: My name is Hannah Holcomb, and that is the way our day is starting at the Holcomb farm outside Canann, Connecticut—the twelfth of May, 1704. I am eleven years old, the eldest girl. My sister Ruth—who you heard whimpering about a little water on her forehead—is ten. Then there are the boys, Joshua and Timothy—

(Joshua Holcomb and Timothy Holcomb enter groggily from right, rubbing the sleep from their eyes.)

Joshua Holcomb: Joshua Holcomb, good day. *(yawns)*

Timothy Holcomb: Timothy Holcomb, beg pardon. *(yawns)*

Hannah Holcomb: Who are nine and eight years old—as well as being the laziest humans in the Colony of Connecticut.

Timothy Holcomb: Beg pardon!

Joshua Holcomb: What did Reverend Ferguson say last Sunday about calling names?

Timothy Holcomb: He spoke for nearly six hours. He must have said something about it.

Hannah Holcomb: And then there is Sarah, the youngest; she is six years old.

(Sarah Holcomb enters from right, bringing a bucket to Ruth; Joshua stands on a stool and mimes stuffing straw into the ceiling.)

Timothy Holcomb: Sarah is not our blood sister. We adopted her when her parents both died of consumption two winters ago.

Hannah Holcomb: We had another sister, Thankful. She died when she was three years old. Our youngest brother, Thomas, died as a baby. Our brother Benjamin is thirteen and apprenticed to Mr. Sims, the silversmith.

Joshua Holcomb: But Sarah is very clever and just about the best candle dipper in the valley! Far better than old "fumble fingers Hannah"!

(Hannah sticks out her tongue at Timothy.)

Hannah Holcomb: I will keep that in mind when I mend your trousers.

Timothy Holcomb: Mother says so, too!

Hannah Holcomb: You see the degree of patience an eldest sister must possess! Everyone to your chores and hurry! You are going to school today!

Joshua Holcomb: I love school!

Timothy Holcomb: I hope my friend Jonathan Whittaker gets to come to school today. He has the biggest cat's eye marble you have ever seen. He got it by trading a wolf claw necklace to Mr. Hawkins, the tinsmith.

Joshua Holcomb: I am going to draw water from the well for mother to cook and wash with. Then I will clean out the milking stalls.

Timothy Holcomb: I am going to sharpen the knife father uses for butchering goats. Then I will chop a cord of wood for the fire.

(Joshua and Timothy exit right.)

Ruth Holcomb: I am going to milk the cow and prepare the washing tub and stitch up a hole in father's vest.

Sarah Holcomb: I am going to feed the chickens and gather eggs for paying my brothers' school bill. And then I will hunt for some wild berries to use in a pie mother is making for the chopping bee next Saturday.

(Ruth and Sarah exit right; Hannah crosses to small table next to fireplace.)

Hannah Holcomb: And I am going to bake the cornbread for dinner. And help mother weed the vegetable garden. And skin the rabbits Joshua shot by the creek—their fur will make a nice pair of work gloves for father.

(Mrs. Holcomb crosses to center and takes an apron from the back of the chair by the table; she ties it on and crosses to fireplace, takes a poker and stirs up the embers; Hannah kneads bread dough.)

Mrs. Holcomb: Ruth is right. It is going to be much more pleasant when we move into the new house. The keeping room will be larger, and the children who now sleep in the attic can sleep on the floor here by the fireplace.

Hannah Holcomb: And the windows will have glass?

Mrs. Holcomb: Now that is only for the wealthy, Hannah. And for the vain who wish to display their wealth to shame their neighbors! Your great-grandparents did not come all this way from England for us to commit such sins of frivolity!

(Mrs. Holcomb takes a cooking pot from the fire and stirs it with a ladle.)

Mrs. Holcomb: Breakfast is ready, children. Come set the table.

(Mr. Holcomb enters from right with Joshua and Timothy following; Mr. Holcomb and Mrs. Holcomb sit at table in the two chairs as Hannah Holcomb puts seven spoons and seven tin cups on the table; Ruth sets a trencher in front of Mr. Holcomb and a second trencher in front of Mrs. Holcomb; Sarah sets a large serving pot at the table center; when everything is ready, the five children stand at attention in front of the table, each holding their spoon.)

Mr. Holcomb: Good morning, all! The porridge and cider smell delicious. Let us say our prayer of thanks. Joshua, you may lead.

Joshua Holcomb: To the Almighty, we thank you for the bounty you have shown to us. Bless this food and our work in preparing it. Amen.

All: Amen.

(Mr. Holcomb and Mrs. Holcomb use their spoons to eat from the two trenchers; the children stand silently.)

Mr. Holcomb: I spoke to Caleb Mifflin the tanner yesterday, as he stopped by the mill to fix a broken wagon wheel. He said the most curious thing: he claimed he saw the Jemisons drinking water with their breakfast.

Mrs. Holcomb: Drinking water! Are they not afraid of disease?

Mr. Holcomb: The Jemisons have some unusual ideas. They use forks, you know. *(dips his fingers into the serving pot)*

Mrs. Holcomb: I have heard that custom is gaining ground with the nobility. And among those in Boston who pretend they are such!

Mr. Holcomb: It will never catch on here. A spoon and a knife is all anyone needs for proper eating.

(Mr. Holcomb and Mrs. Holcomb stand; the children take the two trenchers and begin eating, using spoons and dipping fingers into the serving pot.)

Mr. Holcomb: Now there, use your good manners, children. We have plenty of food to go around. Your mother and sisters see to that. Eat hearty, boys. After you come home from school we have a lot of raking to do in the corn field.

Timothy Holcomb: Sir?

Mr. Holcomb: Yes, Timothy.

Timothy Holcomb: Joshua and I are going to put up our new scarecrow.

Joshua Holcomb: Sir?

Mr. Holcomb: Yes, Joshua.

Joshua Holcomb: It looks just like that clown we saw at Muster Day last year. Do you think the players will come back this year, father?

Mr. Holcomb: I expect so. But we will have to see that all the crops are harvested before we make any promises about entertainments.

Timothy Holcomb & Joshua Holcomb: Yes, sir.

(Mr. Holcomb exits right, followed by Joshua and Timothy; Hannah collects the utensils and serving ware and puts them in a washing pan on the fireplace hearth; Ruth and Sarah rise from table and exit right.)

Mrs. Holcomb: Ruth and Sarah, after you have gathered some wild berries for the cough syrup, you may finish making buttons for father's jacket.

Ruth Holcomb and Sarah Holcomb: Yes, mother.

(Ruth and Sarah exit right.)

Ruth Holcomb: I found a nice patch of mallows growing in a shade patch by the creek—purple and pink.

Sarah Holcomb: They will look pretty in the bonnet I am making for my cornhusk doll.

Mrs. Holcomb: I will go outside and build the fire. Then I will hang the wash kettle over the fire and pour water from the well into the kettle.

Hannah Holcomb: When the water is hot, mother will pour in a helping of lye soap I made last week. And then I take the wash stick and stand at the kettle for two or three hours, pushing and poking the clothes with the wash stick while mother starts getting the food ready for father's mid-day dinner.

Mrs. Holcomb: After I have set some beans to boil and baked up the batch of cornbread Hannah prepared this morning, I will help pound and dry the clothes.

Hannah Holcomb: We take the clothes out of the kettle and lay them out on a battling bench. Then we take big wooden paddles and pound the dirt out of the clothes.

Mrs. Holcomb: Then we rinse the clothes three times to get the soap out and then wring the water out by hand.

Hannah Holcomb: If it does not rain till evening and the wind keeps up, we might be able to get all the clothes dry today.

Mrs. Holcomb: I think the weather today is going to be fine, Hannah. Let us begin!

Hannah Holcomb: I wonder if someday they will ever make a mechanical device that washes and dries clothes?

Mrs. Holcomb: You have such an imagination! Why, I am sure they will invent a device that flies in the air first!

(Mrs. Holcomb and Hannah exit right; at left, Mr. Murray sits behind writing desk; Timothy Holcomb sits on bench, holding a hornbook in hand.)

Mr. Murray: We are a small number today. The Devereaux twins are ill with the grippe. Master Whittaker has to help this father with planting. And with all the rain, the Vanderstel family probably cannot get their wagon across the muddy roads.

Timothy Holcomb: *(raises hand)* Mr. Murray?

Mr. Murray: Yes, Master Holcomb?

Timothy Holcomb: They should forget the old wagon and try walking. They live a couple miles closer than us, and we walk six miles to school and back every day!

Mr. Murray: We are all very impressed by your dedication to scholarship, Master Holcomb. When I was a boy in Scotland, we had no school buildings at all. We met by the roadside in small gaps among the hedge rows that divided the fields. There was not one book among us, but we learned Greek, Latin, French, and etiquette.

(Joshua Holcomb enters from left carrying a bucket of water with a dipper, which he places up left.)

Mr. Murray: Thank you for gathering the water and firewood, children. Please take up your reading books. Master Timothy, would you recite the lesson?

(Timothy Holcomb stands, peering at the hornbook with difficulty and struggling to focus.)

Mr. Murray: Is there a problem, Master Holcomb?

Timothy Holcomb: Sir, it is very dark, and I cannot see the words very clear.

Mr. Murray: Clearly—use the adverb, please. Yes, it is indeed a very dark day, and our window is very small. You may move closer to the fire, Master Holcomb.

Timothy Holcomb: Thank you, Sir.

(Timothy moves closer to the fire and begins to read slowly from hornbook.)

Timothy Holcomb: "The letter D. A Dog will bite a thief at night."

Mr. Murray: Repeat, please, this time from memory.

Timothy Holcomb: The letter D. A Dog will bite a thief at night.

Mr. Murray: That is very good, Master Holcomb. You may sit down. With only three months to a school term, there are many areas of learning we will not have time to fully explore. Reading, writing, and a knowledge of prayers and manners are the most important for general knowledge, and to these we have given much attention. However, in the years to come, an understanding of science will be necessary. I have come into possession of a recent book by Isaac Newton, *Mathematical Principles of Natural Philosophy.* In future lesssons, we will perform some of the experiments he has proposed that involve an element he calls "gravity." Now, let us prepare for our writing lesson.

(Joshua raises his hand.)

Joshua Holcomb: Mr. Murray?

Mr. Murray: Yes, Master Joshua.

Joshua Holcomb: We have run out of bark for our writing slates.

Mr. Murray: *(sighs)* Very well. Go to the willow grove and fetch your bark!

(Mr. Murray follows Timothy and Joshua Holcomb offstage left; Mrs. Holcomb and Hannah enter and sit at the table; they are sewing and mending clothes.)

Mrs. Holcomb: This has been a hard year on clothes. Both boys have grown so much, I have had to make almost twice the number of shirts I made the two years previous. It seems like I am always making or mending clothes.

Hannah Holcomb: Making a shirt is no easy task. Father has to trade a pig for enough wool, then mother cards and spins the wool and weaves and sews the entire shirt, from collar to tail—even making the buttons by hand!

Mrs. Holcomb:	The last two shirts I made for the boys were a nice warm brown color. I made the dye from walnut hulls Hannah found by the creek. Hannah, your dress is getting a bit frayed at the hem. We might cut it back for Ruth to wear.
Hannah Holcomb:	Then I might have a new dress of my own?
Mrs. Holcomb:	Probably one of my old ones until I have time to make something new.
Hannah Holcomb:	We never waste any clothing in this family. When mother's dress wears, she cuts it back to fit me. Then it gets cut again for my younger sisters. When they wear it through, it gets cut into dish rags. And when they get too thin, we weave the strips into rag rug like that one there. *(points to floor)*

(Joshua, Timothy, Ruth, and Sarah Holcomb rush in from right and gather around the main table.)

Sarah Holcomb:	It is really beginning to rain! Cats and dogs!
Mrs. Holcomb:	And oxen, too! Those last few drops felt like hail stones!
Ruth:	Was father able to fix the leak over my bed?
Hannah:	Yes, he did, right after dinner.
Mrs. Holcomb:	I expect we will have an early supper so father can get in a longer day of work tomorrow. Tend to your chores now, while I get the fire ready for cooking.

(Mrs. Holcomb crosses to center and ties on her apron; at the fireplace, she takes a poker and stirs up the embers.)

Timothy Holcomb:	After we finish our afternoon chores, we are free to have fun!
Joshua Holcomb:	Timothy caught a possum last week.
Timothy Holcomb:	Tried to make it a pet, but it ran away.
Joshua Holcomb:	Fishing is always fun. Timothy and I catch plenty of fish—even without a pole!
Timothy Holcomb:	You just slap up the water with your hands till the fish get scared and jump into a frog hole on the bank.
Joshua Holcomb:	All you have to do then is reach in and pull out your fish!
Timothy Holcomb:	And hope no water moccasin is in that hole, too!
Ruth Holcomb:	Sarah and I make dolls.
Sarah Holcomb:	Sometimes father lets us use his hunting knife, and we carve wooden toys.
Ruth Holcomb:	We play ninepins and hide-the-thimble.

Sarah Holcomb:	On nice days we have picnics and go berry-picking.
Joshua Holcomb:	And pitch horse shoes. *(flings an imaginary shoe toward audience)*
Timothy Holcomb:	At night after supper, we often play leapfrog.
Ruth Holcomb:	And twirl-a-top.
Sarah Holcomb:	And ring-around-the-rosy and pop-the-whip and statue. *(points at Ruth)* Freeze!

(Ruth freezes in a silly position.)

Joshua Holcomb:	I am known as one of the best marble shooters in the county!
Timothy Holcomb:	Pshaw! And one of the biggest tall-tale tellers!
Sarah Holcomb:	Storytelling is one of our favorite things. Father and mother have some wonderful stories about growing up on the sea coast in Massachusetts.
Ruth Holcomb:	And riddles. *(to Sarah)* Four fingers and a thumb, yet flesh and bone I have none?
Sarah Holcomb:	A glove! *(to Timothy)* What is red and blue and purple and green? No one can reach it, not even a queen?
Timothy Holcomb:	A rainbow in the sky, the last I have seen! *(to Joshua)* What flies forever, rests never, and is never caught?
Joshua Holcomb:	The wind, the wind, or so I thought. *(to Ruth)* What was born when the world was made, but older than a month never grows?
Ruth Holcomb:	The moon up above; why, look how it glows! *(to Hannah)* Tell me, sister dear, what has a heart in its head?
Hannah Holcomb:	You must mean lettuce—green, purple, or red.
Mrs. Holcomb:	Come now, children. Exercise your hands as well as your tongues. The Baldwins have just had a new baby boy, and we must make a groaning cake for the christening. I need help chopping apples.

(Ruth, Sarah, Joshua, and Timothy surround Mrs. Holcomb.)

Ruth, Sarah, Joshua, Timothy: I can help! Let me! Let me!
(Hannah steps to down center and addresses audience.)

Hannah Holcomb:	Children! I was once that silly, I suppose. But it is a new century, and I think a person—even if she is a girl—should have a mind for more serious matters. I think someday I should like to live in a town like Hartford, or even Boston. And go to university. Or even teach at one! See you on the green!

CURTAIN

July 4, 1776: America's First Birthday

Summary:

On July 4, 1776, Philadelphia citizens discuss the pros and cons of breaking away from England as the Declaration of Independence is signed inside Independence Hall.

Historical Background:

The signing of the Declaration of Independence on July 4, 1776, is one of the most important milestones in the evolution of democracy. It marked the birth of the United States as a nation whose government would be determined by ordinary people and not an elite ruling dynasty.

John Dunlap, a Philadelphia printer, produced the first printed text of the Declaration of Independence. The next day John Hancock, the president of the Continental Congress, began sending copies of the Declaration to political and military leaders throughout the colonies. General George Washington ordered that his personal copy of the Declaration be read to the assembled American army ready to defend New York. At the end of the war, Washington brought his copy home to Mount Vernon. Today, Washington's copy is held in the Library of Congress in Washington, D.C., and is one of only twenty-four copies known to exist.

Pre- or Post-Play Activities:

- Some portions of the dialogue in this play are actually quotations from the Declaration of Independence. Read the dialogue, highlighting sections that you think might be from the original Declaration. Check your highlighted sections against a copy of the document.

- Thomas Jefferson wrote several drafts of the Declaration before the final draft signed by the Continental Congress on July 4. Find a copy of an earlier draft and compare it with the words of the final draft. Make a list of some of the changes. Select one of the changes and write a paragraph explaining why you think that change was made.

- The signers of the Declaration of Independence came from many diverse backgrounds and occupations. What were some of these occupations? Select at least ten signers of the Declaration and do some research to find out what occupations each of them held. Share your findings in a classroom chart.

- It is estimated that one-third of American colonists in 1776 supported the Revolution, one-third remained loyal to King George, and one-third were undecided which side to choose. Are there political issues today that divide Americans in equal numbers? Read a newspaper to identify such an issue. Do a short oral presentation defining the issue and explaining why you feel that it is so important.

- John Adams predicted the signing of the Declaration would be celebrated by Americans for many years to come. What are some of the ways your community celebrates the Fourth of July? Write a descriptive essay telling about your favorite Fourth of July celebration.

Cast: 21 actors, including at least 10 boys (o) and 5 girls (+)

Polly Frederick, serving girl (+)

Olga Spiegel, serving girl (+)

Liza Duncan, fruit seller (+)

Fletcher Tillison, newspaperman (o)

Gordon Hanbury, Loyalist (o)

Jenny Stiles, boarding house owner (+)

Rebecca Parker, Quaker (+)

6 Congressional Delegates

Thomas Jefferson (o)

Benjamin Franklin (o)

Roger Sherman (o)

John Adams (o)

Robert Livingston (o)

Richard Henry Lee (o)

Charles Thomson (o)

John Hancock (o)

Stage Set:

No set is required; however, if desired, a scrim could be mounted behind the stage or off to the side to show slides of 1776 Philadelphia and the Revolutionary Period.

Props:

• Several sheets of writing paper
• Wooden basket with a dozen apples
• 2 quills
• A piece of parchment
• Small wooden writing desk
• Ink pot

Costumes:

Characters wear basic attire of 1770s colonial city-dwellers with accessories relating to their occupation and social status.

For females—a fitted top with below-elbow sleeves and floor-length dirndl skirt in primary colors or gingham pattern; white bonnet or flat-brimmed hat (for Jenny Stiles) or cap (for Liza Duncan) and white single-layer muslin or lace-like scarf (for Polly Frederick and Olga Spiegel); low-heeled shoes with or without metal buckles or clogs. Costumes may be accessorized with colored ribbons on bonnet, hair, top. As a Quaker, Rebecca Parker's attire would be more plain and less colorful, and she might also wear a shopkeeper's apron.

For males—loose-fitting, unlined coat (red, blue, or green) with metal buttons; loose-fitting, lined vest with low armholes and bottom flaps; oversized, pullover white shirt with collar; below mid-knee pants or breeches; white knee-length stockings and low-heeled shoes with or without metal buckles, clogs, or knee boots; tri-corner hat (brown, gray, or black). Fletcher Tillison would wear a simpler outfit, Gordon Hanbury and the Congress members more expensive attire befitting their higher social status.

Staging Helps

Make a tri-corner hat!

Materials

- Hat pattern (at right)
- Black construction paper
- Scissors   • Stapler

Directions

1. Trace pattern onto construction paper three times and cut out.
2. Staple ends of pieces together in a triangular shape, sizing to fit head.

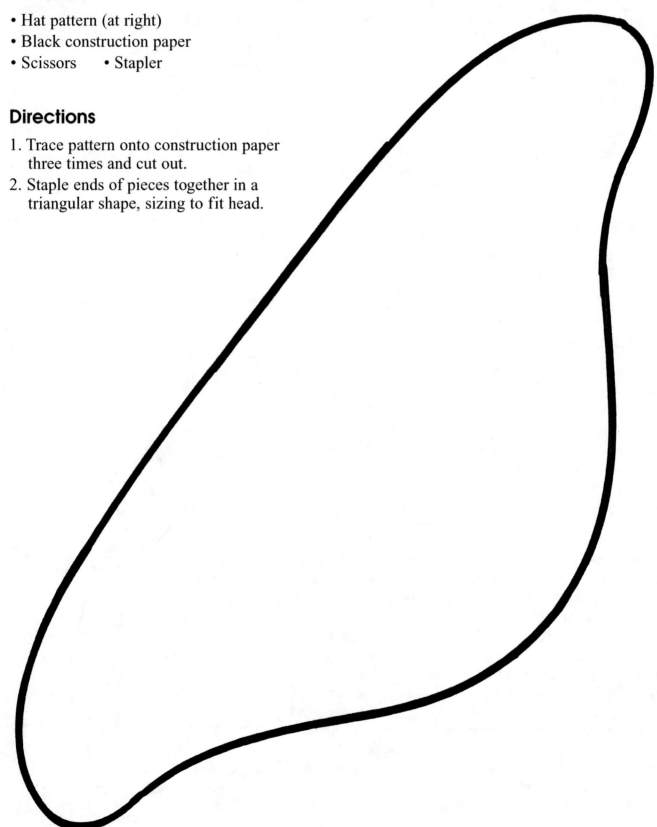

July 4, 1776: America's First Birthday

(As the play begins, Fletcher Tillison, newspaper reporter, stands at down right; he carries writing paper and a quill and pulls his jacket close and his hat over his eyes as he stares up at the sky.)

Fletcher Tillison: Looks like it will be raining shortly—again! Philadelphia in the summer! If you are not wilting with heat, you are drowning in drizzle!

(Liza Duncan enters from right, carrying a basket of apples.)

Liza Duncan: Apples for sale! Picked fresh from the tree at dawn! Red or green. Six for a penny. *(sees Fletcher Tillison)* Good morning, sir! You look like a hard-working sort! How are you on this fine fourth day of July?

Fletcher Tillison: *(bows)* My name is Fletcher Tillison, a reporter for the *Maryland Journal*.

Liza Duncan: *(curtsies)* My name is Liza Duncan, fruit seller for them who be hungry.

Fletcher Tillison: I have just arrived from Baltimore to write a dispatch on the Continental Congress meeting here since May. Have you heard any news?

Liza Duncan: Why, I have never even heard of Baltimore! Is there such a place?

Fletcher Tillison: Madam! You cannot be—

Liza Duncan: *(laughs)* Hold your horses, young man! I am only kidding! If you want news about the Congress, you stand right here at 5th Street and Chestnut. Why, here come the best news-mongers in town!

(Polly Frederick and Olga Spiegel enter from left, cross to down center.)

Liza Duncan: Good morning, ladies!

Polly Frederick: Good morning, Mrs. Duncan. Two apples, please!

Olga Spiegel: *Guten tag, Frau* Duncan! And I will take a half dozen peaches, if you have some.

Liza Duncan:	Polly Frederick and Olga Spiegel, meet Mr. Tillison. He claims he writes for a newspaper in a place called Baltimore!
Fletcher Tillison:	*(bows)* My pleasure. I see you have just come from the Pennsylvania State House. Are you delegates to the Congress?

(Polly Frederick and Olga Spiegel giggle.)

Polly Frederick:	Mr. Tillison, we are serving maids to the Congress!
Liza Duncan:	See what I mean? A keen observer!
Fletcher Tillison:	Have you any news of the Congress? What is it we hear about the writing of a new declaration?
Polly Frederick:	It started last month, June the seventh. Richard Henry Lee, the planter from Virginia, stood before the Congress and gave a resolution.

(Richard Henry Lee enters from left, stands at down left.)

Richard Henry Lee:	These United Colonies are, and of right ought to be, free and independent States. They should be absolved from all allegiance to the British Crown!
Olga Spiegel:	*Ja,* and nine of the colonies said they wanted to be free right away.
Polly Frederick:	Pennsylvania and South Carolina opposed it. The delegates from Delaware could not make up their minds, and the New Yorkers said they had to wait for instructions from their Governor.
Fletcher Tillison:	What happened then?
Olga Spiegel:	On June the eleventh, Congress appointed a committee of five delegates to take *Herr* Lee's ideas and put them into writing.
Polly Frederick:	There was Benjamin Franklin from Philadelphia.

(Benjamin Franklin enters from left, joins Lee at down left.)

Fletcher Tillison:	The scientist and ambassador to England?
Polly Frederick:	Seventy years old and as spry as any man half his age!
Olga Spiegel:	*Ja,* and Roger Sherman of Connecticut. A shoemaker and very strict Puritan.

(Roger Sherman enters from left, joins Lee and Franklin, at down left.)

Polly Frederick:	Robert Livingston of New Jersey, the wealthy aristocrat who started King's College in New York.

(Robert Livingston enters from left, joins Lee, Franklin, and Sherman at down left.)

Fletcher Tillison:	What about John Adams, the lawyer from Boston?

(John Adams enters from left, joins Lee, Franklin, Sherman, and Livingston down left.)

Olga Spiegel: Oh, *ja,* he would not let anything happen without his being right in the middle of it!

John Adams: Gentlemen, there is no time to waste. British troops are even now massing to attack New York. We must make our position on independence absolutely clear.

Benjamin Franklin: Then I suggest we obtain the services of a very clear thinker: Mr. Thomas Jefferson.

(Thomas Jefferson enters from left, joins Lee, Franklin, Sherman, Livingston, and Adams at down left.)

Polly Frederick: A tall, young Virginian with bright red hair just come to town!

Fletcher Tillison: I have heard of Jefferson. He is an architect and inventor, I believe.

(Jenny Stiles enters from right.)

Jenny Stiles: I can tell you all about Mr. Jefferson!

Liza Duncan: Good morning, Mrs. Stiles! Care for an apple?

Jenny Stiles: Mr. Jefferson stays in a room on the second floor of my boarding house. Shy sort of fellow. You can barely squeeze a "Good morning" out of him. Stays up in his room working on a piece of writing. You can hear his quill scratching at the paper day and night, like a squirrel cracking an acorn!

Polly Frederick: They say he works at a special desk he made himself.

(Delegates #1 and #2 enter from left, carrying a small writing desk and stool they set at down left; Jefferson sits at desk, takes out writing paper, quill, and ink pot from inside and begins writing; Delegates #1 and #2 exit left.)

Jenny Stiles: Of course, he does. He is an inventor, after all.

(Rebecca Parker enters from left.)

Jenny Stiles: Ah, my neighbor, Rebecca Parker, the Quaker widow. Friend Parker! And how goes your dry goods shop on Chestnut Street?

Rebecca Parker: Very well, considering the trouble that riseth in the land. Our colonies from Georgia to New England are in an uproar! Citizens mounting arms against the king! Querulous talk of revolution!

Fletcher Tillison: What are your views on the uprising against King George, Mrs. Parker?

Rebecca Parker: My Quaker faith does not condone violence under any cirucmstances. Yet, the tyranny of the king is perhaps a greater violence.

Jenny Stiles:	We have no choice! Said King George himself, "The die is cast. The colonies must triumph or submit."

(Gordon Hanbury enters from left.)

Gordon Hanbury:	Tsk-tsk, more street corner gossip! What sort of idleness is this?
Liza Duncan:	Spoken like a true Tory!

(Gordon Hanbury ignores Liza Duncan, shakes hands with Fletcher Tillison.)

Gordon Hanbury:	Mr. Gordon Hanbury, owner of South Street Imports, at your service.
Fletcher Tillison:	Have you heard about this declaration of independence?
Gordon Hanbury:	Declaration of nonsense! Young man, I greatly value liberty—for it is God's greatest gift to mankind. But I think you will find this armed revolt against the king has very little support from our prosperous merchant class.
Jenny Stiles:	And I think you will find your merchant class shall soon no longer be prosperous, or possessed of liberty!
Polly Frederick:	Mr. Jefferson said almost that very thing to the committee!
Thomas Jefferson:	*(at desk)* The tree of liberty must be refreshed from time to time with the blood of its patriots. We must define our principles of revolution as an exercise of just power.
Roger Sherman:	There are some who will see this declaration as treason.
Richard Henry Lee:	It is a charter of freedom!
John Adams:	To bite the generous hand that has fed us these many years would be considered folly by many. Yet, it is the King of England who has declared war upon his colonies.
Robert Livingston:	Then this declaration should say exactly what the king has done to harm us.
Roger Sherman:	There should be a list of grievances that explain our position.
Thomas Jefferson:	Starting with this one—"The King has refused to Assent to Laws, the most wholesome and necessary for the public good."
Robert Livingston:	Calling King George a law breaker? As if he were a common criminal!
Benjamin Franklin:	As my good friend Poor Richard says, "If your head is made of wax, do not walk in the sun."

(Livingston, Sherman, Jefferson, Lee, Adams laugh.)

Olga Speigel:	Mr. Jefferson wrote the declaration in sixteen days. On June 28, he

presented it to the Congress for debate.

Polly Frederick: And a powerful warm debate it was!

(Polly Frederick and Olga Spiegel carry their apples into the Congress at down left, giving the apples to the delegates, then standing behind in waiting position.)

Benjamin Franklin: *(picks up a paper from the desk, reads)* The Southern states will not accept this point about slavery.

Robert Livingston: We do not ask the planters to give up their slaves, merely to recognize that slavery is an offense against human nature.

Roger Sherman: And that in denying life and liberty to the colonies, King George has treated us as slaves!

Richard Henry Lee: There are several thousand slaves living in the North as well. Many of those delegates will feel uneasy about such a clause.

(John Adams takes quill and scratches on the paper.)

John Adams: For the sake of unity, until we can form a federal government, may we put the matter of slavery aside?

Thomas Jefferson: Very well. Would the Congress care to suggest any other mutilations? Pardon me, "changes"?

Fletcher Tillison: And so two days ago, July the second, Congress took a vote on the declaration?

Gordon Hanbury: Yes, and they accepted, the fools! Now the greatest army in the world will crush us into dust! This Congress is filled with idiots!

Rebecca Parker: Speak for yourself, Friend Hanbury. This Congress is filled with men of courage and wisdom. And they are your neighbors.

(Charles Thomson, John Hancock, and Delegates #1-6 enter from left and gather around Jefferson's desk.)

Jenny Stiles: They are merchants, like you, and doctors and farmers.

Liza Duncan: They came from Scotland, England, Ireland, Wales, and throughout the thirteen American Colonies.

Rebecca Parker: Wealthy planters alongside men who started life in the poorest of means.

Fletcher Tillison: Teachers and clergy, carpenters and ship owners, I hear. Quite a variety.

(Polly Frederick dashes over from Congress.)

Polly Frederick: The secretary, Charles Thomson, is just finishing reading the document aloud!

(Charles Thomson receives a piece of parchment from Thomas Jefferson and reads from it.)

Charles Thomson: "And for the support of this declaration, with a firm reliance on the protection of divine providence, we mutually pledge to each other our lives, our fortunes, and our sacred honor."

(Street characters gaze across stage as if looking into windows at the Congress; Olga Spiegel comes over from Congress as Charles Thomson puts parchment on desk.)

Gordon Hanbury: Who is that taking up the quill?

Olga Speigel: It is John Hancock, president of the Congress and delegate from Massachusetts.

Jenny Stiles: Is he going to sign?

Gordon Hanbury: He takes his life in his hands, if he does!

(John Hancock signs parchment with a bold flourish, stands back and announces loudly.)

John Hancock: There! I guess King George will be able to read that!

(Delegates chuckle as John Hancock hands quill to Benjamin Franklin.)

Delegate #1: *(to Benjamin Franklin)* Mr. Franklin, you are apt to suffer great loss if you sign this document. Do you not fear the wrath of King George?

Benjamin Franklin: Gentleman, if we do not hang together as patriots, we most certainly will hang separately as traitors.

(Delegates chuckle as Delegate #2 steps forward, takes quill and signs.)

Charles Thomson: From New Hampshire, Josiah Bartlett.

Delegate #2: When in the course of human events, it becomes necessary for one people to dissolve the political bonds which have connected them with another …

Delegate #3: And to assume among the powers of the earth, the separate and equal station to which the laws of nature and of nature's God entitle them …

Delegate #4: A decent respect to the opinions of mankind requires that they should declare the cause which impel them to the separation.

Delegate #5: We hold these truths to be self-evident:

Delegate #6: That all men are created equal. . .

Delegate #1: That they are endowed by their Creator with certain unalienable rights …

Delegate #2:	That among these are life, liberty, and the pursuit of happiness.
Delegate #3:	That to secure these rights, governments are instituted among men, deriving their just powers from the consent of the government.
Delegate #4:	That whenever any form of government becomes destructive of these ends, it is the right of the people to alter or to abolish it …
Delegate #5:	And to institute new government, laying its foundation on such principles …
Delegate #6:	And organizing its powers in such form, as to them that shall seem most likely to effect their safety and happiness.

(Delegate #2 places quill in ink pot; Delegates and Congress Members disperse, walk across stage, mingle with other characters from street; Polly Frederick and Olga Spiegel move to down center.)

Polly Frederick:	Those fifty-six men are the bravest men in the whole world, I'll wager.
Olga Spiegel:	And what if the colonies lose the war? Do you think this declaration will be remembered in the years to come?

(John Adams passes by, overhears her remark.)

John Adams:	Remembered? Young miss, this day will be the most memorable in the history of America! It will be celebrated by succeeding generations as a great anniversary, with solemn acts of devotion to God almighty, and with pomp and parade—shows, games, sports, bells, and bonfires—from one end of this continent to the other, from this time forward, forevermore. And to that, I will sign my name again and again!
Delegates #1-6:	Huzzah!
Polly Frederick:	To America and her freedom!
All:	Huzzah!
Olga Spiegel:	To freedom everywhere!
All:	Huzzah! Huzzah! Huzzah!

CURTAIN

Valley Forge:
Turning Point of the Revolution

Summary:

The Colonial Army survives the terrible winter of 1777-78 at Valley Forge to emerge stronger than ever.

Historical Background:

Armies in the 18th century typically stopped fighting during the coldest months to take up winter quarters. During the winter of 1777-78, the British Army stayed warm in the city of Philadelphia while the Continental Army was forced to live in the open woods and fields of Valley Forge, twenty-five miles northwest of the city. The Continentals suffered great hardships, and many thought they would surrender or vanish when it came time to resume the campaign in the spring. However, with remarkable leadership from General Washington and timely help from Prussian and French allies, the Army came through the winter better trained and better equipped than when it arrived. Before Valley Forge, the Colonial soldier was considered a crude amateur; after Valley Forge, he was respected as a skilled warrior equal to any in the world.

Pre- or Post-Play Activities:

- When the modern girl and boy find a diary of a Continental Army soldier, they get a vivid picture of what a real soldier's life was like in that time and place. Find examples of other diaries or first-hand accounts of historical figures and events (*The Diary of Anne Frank, Up from Slavery*, etc.). What details or viewpoints do they use to make you feel as if you were there with the characters? Make a list of at least five of these details and share them with your classmates.

- More soldiers died in the American Revolution from disease than from combat. Make a list of diseases common to the late 1700s and some of the treatments used to cure them.

- Two years after Valley Forge, Major André would be hung as a spy and Peggy Shippen would marry Benedict Arnold, the American general who turned traitor and fought for the British. But in the spring of 1778, it seemed as if England was going to win the war. If you were a colonist, which side would you have supported? Give a short speech explaining why.

- Soldiers from several other countries fought in the American Revolution. What were some of these countries? Within a small group, assign students to represent the foreign soldiers. Role-play a conversation between the soldiers discussing the Revolutionary cause.

Cast: 13 actors, 7 boys (○) and 6 girls (+)

Sam Woodford (○)
Martha Washington (+)
General George Washington (○)
General William Howe (○)
Peggy Shippen (+)

Alexander Hamilton (○)
Patrick O'Moylan (○)
Sarah Potts (+)
Mrs. Loring (+)

Dr. James Thatcher (○)
Lucy Potts (+)
Deborah Hewes (+)
Major André (○)

Stage Set:

No set is required; however, if desired, a scrim could be mounted behind the stage or off to the side to show slides of Valley Forge, George Washington, American Revolution battles, etc.

Props:

• Tattered, cloth-bound diary
• Hand-held video game
• Shovel

• Tin cup
• Basket

Costumes:

Jason and Jennifer wear contemporary American school clothes. Lucy Potts, Sarah Potts, Deborah Hewes, and Martha Washington wear a fitted top with below-elbow sleeves and floor-length dirndl skirt in primary colors or gingham pattern; white bonnet or flat-brimmed hat or cap and white single-layer muslin or lace-like scarf, low-heeled shoes with or without metal buckles or clogs. Mrs. Loring and Peggy Shippen wear gowns accessorized with colored ribbons on bonnet, hair; Sam Woodford and Patrick O'Moylan wear Continental Army uniform—blue coats with white lapels, red cuffs and white buttons, white or beige leggings, and tattered low-heeled shoes. General George Washington and Alexander Hamilton wear similar basic uniform but with epaulettes and tri-cornered cockade hats and black leather knee-length boots; General William Howe and Major André wear red coats with white lapels, white cuffs and silver buttons, white leggings, and black leather knee-length boots. Dr. James Thatcher wears loose-fitting, unlined black coat over white shirt with collar, below mid-knee pants or breeches with front waist/leg bands and trim held together with clasp or button; white knee-length stockings and low-heeled shoes with or without metal buckles, clogs, or knee boots; tri-corner hat (brown, gray, or black— see directions on page 30).

Pronunciation Guide:

Schuylkill — **Skoo**-kul
Von Steuben — Von **Stoo**-bin

Staging Helps

Uniform Coat

Except for color, the uniform coats of the British army and the Revolutionary army were much the same. Follow these directions to make simple coats for military characters to wear.

Materials

- Paper grocery bag
- Scissors
- Red and blue tempera paint
- Paint brush
- Gold braid trim
- Glue

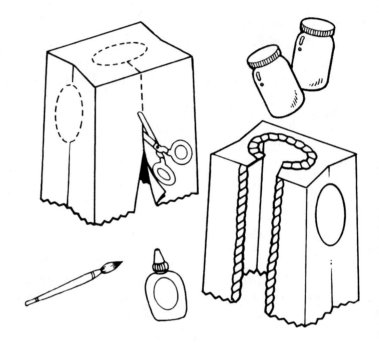

Directions

1. Cut up the front center of bag. Cut neck and arm openings, as illustrated.
2. Paint bag red or blue.
3. Glue gold braid around front and neck openings to decorate.

Mob Cap

For everyday wear, many women in the colonial and revolutionary eras wore a simple cloth cap called a mob cap.

Materials

- 24-inch (61 cm) square of fabric
- Seam binding
- Elastic
- Needle and thread

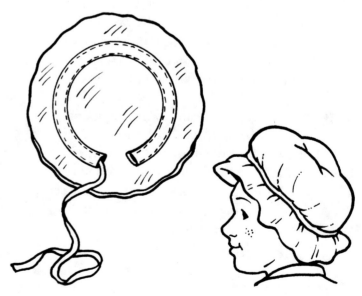

Directions

1. Cut a large circle from the fabric.
2. Sew a casing of seam binding two inches (5 cm) from the edge of the circle.
3. Measure elastic to fit child's head plus one inch (2.5 cm).

Valley Forge: Turning Point of the Revolution

(As the play begins, Jason stands at down right, playing with a hand-held video game; Jennifer sees him and frowns.)

Jennifer: Jason! Come on, you'll miss the tour!

Jason: Sorry! Hold on, Jen, I've almost vanquished the entire solar system!

Jennifer: Why are you playing with toys when we're in this incredible museum?

Jason: Because everything in this place is boring. It doesn't move, it doesn't interact. It's just old stuff! Like that old prom jacket. *(points)*

Jennifer: That's a Continental Army uniform. The soldier who wore it might have seen George Washington. Or even talked to him!

Jason: Right, like he's going to pop in the door anytime soon. I'm sorry, Jennifer, but I don't see how knowing all this history is going to help me invent a new video game system that makes me a zillionaire by high school. I—hey, what are you doing?

(Jennifer has spotted something on the ground a few feet upstage; she bends down and picks it up; it is a small tattered, cloth-bound book.)

Jennifer: It's a book!

Jason: Oh. Somebody must have dropped it from the gift shop. Better take it back.

Jennifer: Looks really old. *(leafs through pages)* It's a diary! Somebody's private diary.

Jason: *(examines book)* It's got maps and sketches. Look at those little curlicue letters.

Jennifer: I don't think this came from the gift shop.

Jason: *(points)* Here's the first page. *(reads)* "My name is Samuel Elijah Woodford. Most people call me Sam. I am sixteen years old and was born on a farm in Burlington County, New Jersey. That is where I have lived all my life, until this war began and I joined the army of General Washington, the army of the United States of America, I am proud to say. But on this day of December 20, 1777—"

(Jason stops and looks at Jennifer; Sam Woodford enters from left.)

Sam Woodford: That pride could sure use a hot cup of cocoa to perk it up.

(Sam Woodford steps to down left, lays down his bundle and musket; he looks around.)

Sam Woodford: We have just arrived at our winter quarters, a place called Valley Forge. It is twenty-five miles northwest of Philadelphia—a distance the British will not easily cover in one day's march—so we feel safe from surprise attack. *(shivers)* Our real enemy is the weather. After crossing the Schuylkill River on the wobbliest bridge I have ever seen, we were forced to camp in the snow for five days when a blizzard blocked the road. We have had nothing to eat for two or three days except what the trees of the forests and fields afforded us. Tonight for supper, we will have the ration Congress has granted each soldier—half a cup of rice and a tablespoon of vinegar. *(raises cup in toast)* Merry Christmas!

(Jennifer and Jason kneel at down right, reading through book.)

Jason: This is incredible! It's as if this Sam Woodford guy was right there at Valley Forge!

Jennifer: Of course he was! *(points to page)* He mentions George Washington and one of his aides, Alexander Hamilton.

(General George Washington enters from left with Alexander Hamilton by his side.)

Alexander Hamilton: General, if I may say so, you have chosen an excellent defensive position. *(points out to audience)* One side is protected by the river. Two shallow creeks provide natural barriers against cavalry and artillery. The high plateau means any attackers would have to charge uphill. And all of it surrounded by rich farm country!

George Washington: Thank you, Captain Hamilton. Unfortunately, the British visited the village two weeks ago. They have burned everything they could not steal. We are left with trees and mud, not a single chicken, cow, or ear of corn.

(Deborah Hewes enter from left, carrying a basket.)

Deborah Hewes: General Washington! My name is Deborah Hewes. I live in the house overlooking Valley Creek. The house is made of stone, so the redcoats could not burn it. You are welcome to use it as your quarters.

George Washington: We will pay you one hundred pounds Pennsylvania currency for its rental. Unlike the enemy, we do not steal from our citizens.

Deborah Hewes: And please accept this basket of corn bread and summer squash. It is all we have left from the British raid.

George Washington: *(bows)* You are most kind. *(gestures to Sam Woodford)* Private! Take these supplies to the commissary.

Sam Woodford: Yes, General. *(takes the basket)*

George Washington: *(to Deborah Hewes)* This soldier will accompany you safely home.

(Deborah Hewes curtseys and exits left, followed by Sam Woodford.)

Alexander Hamilton: General, we have nine thousand men and only a handful of wooden huts for shelter.

George Washington: Luckily, we have plenty of canvas. Set the enlisted men to sewing and putting up tents. They will be easier to keep clean, and we shall need every stick of wood for fuel. And I will write Congress—again!—and demand they send the food, clothing, and weapons they've been promising for months!

Alexander Hamilton: The Congress still wishes us to attack General Howe in Philadelphia?

George Washington: I sometimes believe Congress wishes us to commit suicide! Look around, Captain! This is an army of skeletons! Howe has fifteen thousand troops, well-fed and rested. If I were he, I would send us into oblivion, like swatting a fly from a tea cup!

(General Washington and Alexander Hamilton exit left; General William Howe, Major André and Mrs. Loring enter from up left and cross to down center; Mrs. Loring is arm-in-arm with General Howe.)

Major André: General Howe, what is left of the rebel army is stuck in a field no more than a day's march north. They are ill-equipped, half-starved, and frozen. One quick foray, and we could end the war!

General Howe: Major André, this war will dribble out on its own accord. Indeed, Washington's army will not last the winter. By spring, those who have not deserted will be fit only to surrender.

Major André: But, General—

Mrs. Loring: Major, you have only just arrived. Do you not wish to enjoy the hospitality of our fair city?

General Howe: Mrs. Loring, your Philadelphia hospitality is legendary. I have heard much of your wonderful pageants and dances!

Mrs. Loring: And our taverns serve the most delightful delicacies!

Major André: But our duty, General—

General Howe: Major, our duty is to preserve the colonies for King George. If we do so without excessive loss of life, so much the better. These rebels are, after all, our own kinsmen, our own friends and neighbors. *(smiles at Mrs. Loring)* While we stay warm and toasty, let them chip away at their ice cubes!

(General Howe and Mrs. Loring laugh, exit left, with Major André following, shaking his head and frowning.)

Jennifer: *(reads from book)* "December 26. We awoke to find four inches of new snow on the ground."

(Sam Woodford is on the ground at down center, waking and shivering, huddled in a thin, tattered blanket.)

Jennifer: *(reads from book)* "Breakfast was a cold meal of cold water and fire cakes—a slab of flour and water batter fried on a griddle. That would also be our lunch, supper, and tomorrow's breakfast as well."

(Patrick O'Moylan enters from left, holding a shovel.)

Sam Woodford: Good morning, Sergeant! And you brought us a Christmas present!

Patrick O'Moylan: Aye, lad, I'm changing me name from Patrick O'Moylan to Jolly St. Nicholas! Up now, all of ye! General Washington wants us digging our cares away!

Sam Woodford: We are the most fortified, dug-in passel of troops in the history of warfare! I bet I have dug eighteen trenches this last week alone!

Patrick O'Moylan: No trenches today, lads. Grave detail. We're burying the horses and men that died in the night.

Sam Woodford: *(takes shovel)* At least all the digging keeps us from losing limbs to frostbite.

(Dr. James Thatcher enters from left, accompanied by Lucy and Sarah Potts.)

Patrick O'Moylan: Top o' the morning, Dr. Thatcher.

Dr. James Thatcher: Good day, gentlemen. This is Mrs. Lucy Potts and her daughter, Sarah. They live across Sullivan's Bridge and are helping me in the field hospital.

Lucy Potts: We are spreading the word to be very careful about your drinking water. We have several new cases of typhus. That, along with the regular dysentery, malaria—pneumonia, of course.

Sarah Potts: General Washington says for every man killed in battle, we lose twenty to disease.

Dr. James Thatcher: Speaking of disease, Sergeant, have your squad report to the hospital at noon for their inoculations.

Sam Woodford: Are you mad? Sticking a needle filled with smallpox into your skin? That is the silliest thing I've ever heard!

Patrick O'Moylan: Easy, lad, it'll sicken you a bit but save you from dying. The general gave it to the troops last winter at Morristown. Many of us are alive this winter because of it. *(to Dr. Thatcher)* I'll see you back to the hospital, sir and misses.

(Patrick O'Moylan, Dr. Thatcher, Lucy Potts and Sarah Potts exit up left; Sam Woodford sighs and starts digging.)

Sam Woodford: January 29, 1778. Not much new to write down. Still digging. Still freezing. Still alive, though, and I often wonder how. The quartermaster says we are liable to receive a shipment of soap today. Each soldier is supposed to receive three ounces of soft soap, and one ounce of hard soap every week for cleaning clothes, quarters, and person. There is not a spare blanket to be found for fifteen miles. And we have been waiting for bread for six days. Last night, the cry was heard throughout the camp …

Offstage Voices: Meat! Meat! For the love of God, give us meat!

Sam Woodford: Yet with all the misery, the men still love General Washington and would follow him anywhere. He spends most of the day and night writing Congress on our behalf.

(General George Washington and Alexander Hamilton enter from left, stand at down left.)

George Washington: Congress has asked us to fight a war but not given us the means to do so. Look about you, Captain! These unfortunate soldiers are in want of everything. They have neither coats nor hats, nor shirts, nor shoes. Their feet and their legs freeze until they are black. From the depths of my soul I pity those miseries, which it is in my power neither to relieve nor prevent. Can the prospects of this new nation be any more bleak than at this dark hour?

Alexander Hamilton: *(holds up a letter)* General, we have a letter of introduction from a new officer, a Baron von Steuben.

George Washington: Is he from the Prussian Army? I have never heard of him.

Alexander Hamilton: The letter is signed by Benjamin Franklin, who appears to have met the Baron while in Paris negotiating with the French. The Baron claims to be an expert in military drill.

George Washington: What salary does he ask?

Alexander Hamilton: *(glances at letter)* Because of his love of liberty and his dislike of

England, the Baron has offered his services gratis.

George Washington: Excellent! Appoint him "Acting Inspector General" and tell him to train the troops in basic maneuvers.

(George Washington and Alexander Hamilton exit left; Sam Woodford puts his shovel over his shoulder like a rifle and begins marching in place.)

Sam Woodford: Turned out that Baron von Steuben was not a real Baron. Just another European officer without a steady job. He did not even speak English, but would shout his orders in French, which the other officers passed on to us in English. But, sakes alive, did he know his close-order drill. He marched us for hours, and the men loved it!

(Patrick O'Moylan enters from left.)

Patrick O'Moylan: Hup one, hup two! Regiment halt! *(mimics German accent)* You vill not be und mob! You vill be an army!

Sam Woodford: The Baron wrote up his own training manual, first of its kind for an American army. And before long, that is just what we were—an army!

Patrick O'Moylan: We were still outnumbered, but the Baron made us into a fighting force that could compete with any troops the British could put in the field.

(Martha Washington enters from up left and crosses to down center.)

Sam Woodford: February 25. Martha Washington arrives and the men are astounded. Yes, the wife of the general himself bunking down with us frozen scarecrows!

Martha Washington: I am just an old-fashioned Virginia housekeeper—steady as a clock, busy as a bee, and cheerful as a cricket! Each morning I conduct needlework sessions with the local women, where we knit and sew supplies for the men. In the afternoon, I visit sick soldiers and help the General with his letters.

Patrick O'Moylan: She calls her husband "the old man"!

Sam Woodford: March 9. Wagons have begun arriving with clothing and food. And today came the strangest sight of all—a regiment of military bakers! Seventy men led by Philadelphia gingerbread baker Christopher Ludwig!

Martha Washington: Mr. Ludwig refused to take a profit from his labor. For the first time all winter, each soldier got the daily pound of bread promised by Congress.

Sam Woodford: April 2. Shad in the river!

(Sarah Potts dashes in from left, carrying a basket.)

Sarah Potts:	Great huge schools of shad are swimming up the river. They call shad a poor man's fish, and before the war, some even refused to put it on the table.
Sam Woodford:	But the men are eating them by the bucketful!
Patrick O'Moylan:	The whole camp stinks of fish, and our fingers are so oily we cannot hold a shovel!
Martha Washington:	With the warming weather, nature sends a silent signal of our revival. Dogwood blossoms!
Sarah Potts:	We arose this morning to the sight of a thousand dogwood trees in full bloom! Gigantic, spectacular white blossoms on the ground, in the air—millions of them!
Sam Woodford:	May 1. More militia have joined, nearly twelve thousand men altogether!
Martha Washington:	Congress has granted the Valley Forge soldiers an extra month's pay for having stuck it out through the miseries of the winter.
Patrick O'Moylan:	We danced around the maypole and serenaded General Washington with a chorus of "Yankee Doodle."
Sam Woodford:	May 6, the best news of all—France is joining the war on our side!

(Sam Woodford, Patrick O'Moylan, Martha Washington, and Sarah Potts cheer and move to down left as General William Howe, Peggy Shippen, and Major André enter from up left and gather at down center.)

Major André:	With the French in the war, we shall have to leave the city immediately!
General Howe:	Now, Major, there is no need to panic. Take a moment and meet Miss Peggy Shippen. She is going to serve as hostess for our next dance.
Peggy Shippen:	It will be the grandest event in Philadelphia's history! You will be our special guest, won't you, Major?
Major André:	We must take immediate action, General. France will give Washington new weapons and new troops. Why, the French fleet could sail up the Delaware and attack us where we stand!
Peggy Shippen:	But, Major, if you move back to New York, all the Philadelphia ladies will be terribly disappointed.
Major André:	General Howe, the urgency—
General Howe:	I will consult with my superiors, Major. Until then, your orders are to remain—at ease!

(General Howe and Peggy Shippen laugh, exit left arm-in-arm, with Major André following, shaking his head and frowning; Sam Woodford rushes in from up left.)

Sam Woodford: June 18. The British have left Philadelphia! General Washington has given the order to pursue! He says we are ready to fight. If we have beaten this cold winter, we can beat the British! So, we spend this last day cleaning up the grounds, burying all our garbage and preparing to chase those redcoats into the ocean!

(Jason and Jennifer stand at down right; the Colonial characters filter onstage behind Sam Woodford.)

Jason: *(closes book)* That's the last entry. I wonder what happened to Sam Woodford after that?

Jennifer: I don't know. But we do know that the Continental Army began to win battles. Valley Forge was the turning point of the Revolution.

Jason: *(peers closely at book)* Say, what's this?

Jennifer: It's a note inside the back cover!

Sam Woodford: *(to audience)* Valley Forge will be remembered as a place of great sacrifice and suffering. But it was also where a new American army was born. Professional, confident, and dedicated to winning our freedom.

All: Huzzah for General Washington! Huzzah for the United States of America! Huzzah!

CURTAIN